Ripley's®

BIRDS of Prey

Written by:
Richie Chevat

With an Introduction by:
Ellen Goldberg
Director of Education
The Raptor Trust

Series Edited by:
Madeline Boskey, Ph.D.

SCHOLASTIC INC.

New York   Toronto   London   Auckland
Mexico City   New Delhi   Hong Kong   Buenos Aires

D1247384

Developed by Nancy Hall, Inc., New York, NY
Designed by Gen Shibuya and Iram Khandwala

Published by Scholastic Inc.,
90 Old Sherman Turnpike, Danbury, Connecticut 06816

Printed in the U.S.A.
First Scholastic printing, February 2004

ISBN 0-439-63360-5

The creators of this book wish to thank Ellen Goldberg of The Raptor Trust
for her invaluable suggestions, advice, and inspiration.

Robert Ripley began his career as a sports cartoonist. One day, he was facing a deadline and couldn't think of anything to draw. Then he had a brainstorm. Digging through his files, Ripley found nine amazing sports facts—and finished his cartoon just in time. Little did he know it would become the first of thousands of Believe It or Not! cartoons.

In time, Ripley expanded his column beyond the subject of sports. He sought out oddities of all kinds—bizarre people, places, things, and events—to share with his readers. Ripley was tireless. His searches took him all over the world. Many of his findings appeared in books and syndicated newspaper columns. Museums known as Odditoriums, located across the globe, display numerous artifacts he collected. The Ripley archives include the remarkable collection that was Robert Ripley's passion.

Ripley loved animals. Not surprisingly, many pieces about animals can be found in the archives. Inspired by Ripley's explorations, Wild World books are designed to give readers a close-up look at the amazing creatures that inhabit the Earth. Some of the most breathtaking creatures of all are birds of prey, also known as raptors. Their size, their speed and grace in flight, and their awesome skill at catching prey inspire our respect. Condors have the largest wingspan of any birds, up to 9 feet (3 m) across. The peregrine falcon is the fastest living creature on—or above—Earth. It can fly at speeds up to 200 miles (322 km) per hour. Owls can fly without making a sound, which is a wonderful advantage for taking prey by surprise. There is so much more to learn—as you will discover in the pages of this book.

Filled with beautiful photography, astounding facts, and original cartoons from the Ripley archives, *Birds of Prey* will amaze you as you encounter these majestic hunters of the sky.

Prepare to experience the awesome world of raptors.

Madeline Boskey, Ph.D.
Series Editor

It is hard to put into words why birds of prey are so wonderful. They are not cute, like penguins. Koalas are cuddly looking, but eagles definitely are not. And raptors don't make you laugh, like otters and seals can. If you are lucky enough to see a peregrine falcon shoot through the sky at 200 miles (322 km) per hour while chasing a pigeon, it is definitely not funny (and certainly not for the pigeon) but it is awe inspiring. People love gorillas and chimpanzees because when we look at them, we recognize many human qualities. When you look into the eyes of a great horned owl, what looks back is a fierce will, an indomitable, unapologetic stare that says: Don't come closer. I may live in your backyard, I may eat the squirrels that live there, but it is my forest and they are my squirrels, and I will not thank you, nor will I look back at you when I fly away.

Besides being magnificent, raptors are important. A barn owl family of two parents raising four babies may eat thousands of mice during nesting season. Young, growing birds of prey sometimes eat their own body weight in food each day. Most hawks and owls thrive on a diet that includes rodents, so they put a big dent in rodent populations. That is bad news for rodents but very good news for humans because no one wants to be overrun with rats and mice. Our local hawks and owls make sure that doesn't happen.

Yet as important as raptors are, they are simply part of their ecosystems and habitats. In a complex ecosystem, every living thing has its own place, from seeds cast into fields to millipedes living under dead wood, from the voles and birds that forage seeds and insects to the eagles, hawks, and owls that eat the voles and birds. And all these living things depend on the health of the forests, the mountains, the deserts, and all the other habitats that are their homes.

What I find most exciting about raptors is that they are dazzling, awe inspiring, thrilling, and, most of all, wild. They belong to the wild world of the dark rain forest, where harpy eagles snag sloths from trees. Birds of prey inhabit the wild world of mountains, where golden eagles soar and try to scare mountain goats off cliffs for an easy meal. Raptors are wild, and when they inhabit cities, as peregrine falcons do in New York City, Montreal, Chicago, and almost every major city in North America, they make our cities "wild," too.

Raptors bring with them the wilderness. You may never see a tiger hunting in your backyard, but you may see a "winged tiger"—a Cooper's hawk or a great horned owl. When you do, you will freeze, hold your breath, and feel the hair on your arms tingle and rise. For that moment, in a flash of wings and feathers, they make you part of their wild world.

Ellen Goldberg
Director of Education
The Raptor Trust
Millington, NJ

Contents

Hunters
of the Sky

Soaring high overhead or swooping down at 200 miles (322 km) per hour, there is nothing as exciting as a hawk, an eagle, or other bird of prey. They are the hunters of the sky.

Although other birds live by hunting—herons catch fish with their long beaks, crows kill and eat small animals, and even sparrows hunt insects—only hawks, eagles, falcons, vultures, owls, and a few other birds are called birds of prey. What sets them apart?

The red-tailed hawk is the most common hawk seen in North America.

The secretary bird swallows its prey whole.

Birds of prey are at the top of the food chain. No other animals hunt them (except for humans). In addition, birds of prey, unlike other birds, kill with their feet. Most hunting birds use their beaks to grab and kill their food. Finally, birds of prey all have a distinctive hook-shaped beak.

The snowy owl can be found in the Arctic.

There are more than 400 species of birds of prey. They come in all sizes. The tiny elf owl, found in North America, weighs only 1.4 ounces (40 g). The California condor, a type of vulture, can weigh as much as 23 pounds (10.4 kg) and can measure more than 9 feet (2.7 m) from wingtip to wingtip.

Birds of prey are found on every continent except Antarctica. Some live in tropical rain forests, some in the deserts, and some, like the snowy owl, live in the Arctic.

The California condor is the largest raptor in North America.

Scientists can learn a lot about the environment by studying birds of prey, like this peregrine falcon.

Birds of prey play an important role in nature's cycle. As predators, they help keep down populations of rodents, for example. If the rodent population is not held in check, their numbers could increase to the point where there would not be enough food for them and they would begin dying of starvation. That kind of situation could lead to the spread of disease.

As scientists monitor birds of prey, changes in their populations and migratory patterns reveal a lot of information—and not only about specific raptor populations. Because raptors are at the top of the food chain, scientists can learn about the health of the entire environment by studying them.

Built for Hunting

A hawk's talons are designed for killing and holding onto prey.

All birds of prey have four toes. In hawks, eagles, and falcons, three point forward and one points backward.

Beaks & Claws

An eagle's beak is fierce looking and sharp, but its deadliest weapon is its feet. Like all birds of prey, the eagle uses its sharp claws, called talons, to kill and catch its food. Its beak is used to tear food into pieces small enough to eat.

Different birds of prey have feet and claws that are adapted to capturing the animals they hunt. Ospreys hunt fish and have spiny skin on the bottom of their feet called spicules to keep slippery fish from wriggling away. Vultures are the only birds of prey that do not have strong claws. Their food is already dead when they find it.

An osprey sits atop its perch.

Putting Its Foot Down

The secretary bird is a raptor that lives in Africa. It can grow to about 5 feet (1.5 m) tall. Instead of flying after its prey, the secretary bird runs after it and uses its large feet to stomp on snakes and other animals.

The harpy eagle of South America has talons that are bigger than a grizzly bear's claws.

Birds of prey are also called raptors. The name comes from the Latin word *rapare*, which means "to seize or carry off."

The black plumes of secretary birds reminded people of quill pens, which were used for writing years ago. That's how these birds got their name.

Eyes Like an Eagle

The expression *eagle-eyed* is no joke. Birds of prey have fantastic vision. Some have eyesight that is eight times better than ours. For example, the wedge-tailed eagle of Australia can see a rabbit from a mile (1.61 km) away.

Bald eagles are powerful hunters. They will also steal food from other birds.

THE NEST OF A BALD EAGLE OFTEN WEIGHS 2 TONS

Raptors' eyes are set closer together on the front of their heads than the eyes of other birds. This helps them judge distances and zero in on prey as they hunt. Hawks, falcons, and eagles also see more shades of color than we do. This helps them to find and catch animals that have camouflage markings. For example, if an animal has a brown pattern that looks like dead leaves, a raptor might be able to see that the animal is a different shade of brown than the leaves around it.

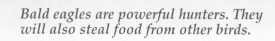

Ospreys are great fishing hawks and are always found near open waters.

Sit or Swoop?

Birds of prey hunt in many different ways. Peregrine falcons soar through the air, looking for small birds below. When they spot one, they fold their wings and dive down, reaching speeds of up to 200 miles (322 km) per hour. They pound their quarry with their feet. Some even make "fists" out of their claws when they strike. Many other birds of prey, like the kestrel, sit quietly on a perch, waiting for a small animal to venture out. Then they swoop down and grab it up in their claws. Eagles do both types of hunting, from perches and from flight.

Whoosh! Swooping in to strike its prey, this peregrine falcon means business.

A Rotten Trick

Except for the turkey vulture, most birds of prey do not have great senses of smell or taste. The turkey vulture can find carrion, or rotting meat, by the smell alone. It can also smell fresh meat at a great distance. Other types of vultures follow the turkey vulture to the carcass and join in the feast.

Vultures, like this bearded vulture, eat carrion, which might sometimes be roadkill!

Broad Wings & Long Tails

Birds of prey come in all shapes and sizes. Hawks that hunt among trees or on the edge of forests, like goshawks, have long tails and short, rounded wings. Their tails help them to switch directions quickly, and their short wings allow them to fly among the trees. Falcons hunt in the open air. They have wings that are long, slender, and pointed to help them go very fast over long distances.

Goshawks fly and hunt for prey among trees and foliage.

THE PEREGRINE FALCON AS A CHICK CAN TAKE AS LONG AS 2 DAYS TO BREAK OUT OF ITS SHELL

Some raptors are long-distance travelers. The Swainson's hawk migrates every year from western North America to Argentina. Raptors, like other land birds, prefer not to migrate over water. To get from North America to South America and back, millions of raptors fly over Central America twice a year. When it comes to migration, hawks have some amazing abilities. Wildlife biologists studying Swainson's hawks think that these hawks may not stop to eat for the entire course of their migration—which can take up to two months and cover a distance of more than 5,000 miles (8,000 km). That's a long time between meals!

Long-Distance Raptors

When flying, the wings of a Swainson's hawk are more pointed than those of other buteos.

A Lot of Hot Air

When you watch a hawk soar overhead without moving its wings, it is riding a thermal, or an updraft of warm air. On a hot, sunny day, the land heats up and hot air currents begin to rise. Birds like hawks and vultures ride those currents into the sky like elevators. Then they glide down, barely flapping a wing. Hawks and other birds migrate by gliding from one thermal to another. Thermals do not form over water—one reason raptors do not migrate over the ocean.

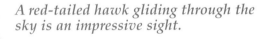

A red-tailed hawk gliding through the sky is an impressive sight.

Birds of Prey, Night or Day

Birds of prey are divided into two main groups. One group is active during the day (diurnal) and includes eagles, hawks, and falcons. Owls make up the second group. Most owls fly and hunt at night (nocturnal), although some are also active at dawn and dusk and some are even active during the day.

Like most owls, the wood owl sees well at night.

Which Came First?

Birds come from eggs. (Or is it the other way around?) Just as birds of prey come in all shapes and sizes, so do their eggs. Owl eggs are almost as round as balls. Eagle eggs are shaped like chicken eggs but are larger. Peregrine falcon eggs are dull red and sometimes speckled. Almost all raptors build their nests in trees.

Scientists study the eggs of condors to learn more about these mighty birds.

THE CALIFORNIA CONDOR HAS A LIFE SPAN OF 100 YEARS

Mates for Life

Eagles, hawks, and many other birds of prey mate for life. Both the male and the female work together to build the nest and care for the young. Usually the female sits on the eggs and the male hunts and brings her food. Once the young are hatched and growing, it may take both parents to catch enough food for them.

Red-shouldered hawks mate for life and return each spring to the same nest to raise a new family.

Raptor Appetites

The larger the raptor, the smaller the percentage of food it needs to eat in relation to its body weight. So a big raptor like a golden eagle at 9 pounds (4 kg) only needs less than 7 percent of its body weight in food to stay alive, which is only half a pound (251 g) of meat a day. However, a small, male sharp-shinned hawk, which may weigh 3.5 ounces (100 g), must eat about 25 percent of its body weight, or just about 1 ounce of food (28 g) to maintain itself.

A golden eagle coming at you!

Girl Power

In many species of animals, the male is bigger than the female. Not so among birds of prey. For example, female sharp-shinned hawks are twice as large as males. Scientists are not sure why this is so. In some raptor species, the size difference means the male and female hunt different food. That means there are two food sources for the pair instead of just one, which increases their odds of getting a good meal.

Sharp-shinned hawks are small, but they can eat prey as large as a blue jay.

THE **CHANTING GOSHAWK** OF SOUTH AFRICA IS THE ONLY BIRD OF PREY *THAT SINGS*

11

Hawks

High-Flying Hawks

The name hawk is used for more than 270 types of birds around the world. The "true hawks," also called accipiters, have short, rounded wings that are perfect for flying among trees. They usually fly and hunt low to the ground. Buteos are the hawks that soar high overhead. They have large, broad wings and broad tails. The Cooper's hawk is a good example of an accipiter. The red-tailed hawk is a buteo.

A red-tailed hawk perches on a fence post for a short rest.

Hawks Are No Heavyweights

Like all birds, hawks have to be lightweight in order to fly. The red-tailed hawk, with a wingspan of 58 inches (1.4 m), weighs only about 2.4 pounds (1.1 kg)! About half of that weight is muscle.

Cooper's hawks are fairly uncommon, but most likely to be seen during fall migrations.

Not Too Picky

Some hawks have very specialized diets. For example, the osprey will only eat fish. Many hawks, however, are not picky eaters. Hawk food includes mice, rabbits, birds, lizards, snakes, and insects. Even a large bird like the red-tailed hawk, which can grow to be almost 2 feet (60 cm) tall, will occasionally hunt and eat insects.

A red-tailed hawk sweeps in to strike its prey.

A red-tailed hawk "mantles" its prey, cloaking it so there is no hope of escape.

Here are some typical prey that are eaten by hawks.

Most buteos are strong fliers. To migrate more than 5,000 miles (8,000 km)— like Swainson's hawks do each fall—they have to be!

Hawk Eyes

One reason hawks are so fierce looking is the sharp, bony ridge above their eyes. They fly at very high speeds while chasing their prey. Their jutting brow helps protect their eyes from getting hurt if they hit a branch or some other object and acts like a visor, protecting their eyes from the sun. Ospreys, which fly over water, don't have a facial ridge, so they don't look as fierce. Hawks also have an extra eyelid called a nictitating membrane, which protects the eye. The membrane often closes just as the bird makes its kill.

The clear extra eyelid of the red-tailed hawk offers extra protection.

The translucent nictitating membrane can be seen clearly in the profile of this ferruginous hawk, the largest of the buteos.

Lots of Pluck

Hawks that hunt birds pluck the feathers off before they eat. In many species, such as the sparrow hawk, the male has a plucking post where he takes his catch to clean it before bringing it to his mate and their young ones in the nest.

American kestrel.

A Swainson's hawk in flight.

A Harris's hawk often perches on fence posts or utility poles.

A hawk chick alone in its nest.

The Family That Preys Together

The Harris's hawk is one of the few raptors that hunts in groups. Close relatives form groups that work as a team. This allows them to kill jackrabbits, which might be larger than any single hawk. For raptor watchers, it also means if one Harris's hawk is visible, there may be others in the vicinity. They are also one of the few hawks that build nests in colonies and help each other feed and raise their young.

Harris's hawks go for the buddy system. They hunt cooperatively.

Go Fly a Kite

These kites are not made out of paper and wood. They are a kind of bird of prey. You can recognize some of these hawklike birds by their forked tails. The swallow-tailed kite has the most extremely forked tail, just like its namesake, the swallow. Some types of kites have adapted very well to human development. For example, the black-shouldered kite is now very common in the southeastern United States.

Kites are great at multitasking. They drink water on the fly, dipping down to a lake or stream for a sip. Some also do their nest building while flying. While in flight, swallow-tailed kites break up small branches to use in their nests.

Many kites eat their food while flying.

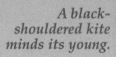

A black-shouldered kite minds its young.

A northern harrier flies in search of food in the grass below.

The snail kite of Florida eats only one type of snail. It has a curved bill that allows it to pry its food out of the shell.

A northern harrier flaps and glides over marshes.

Hovering Harriers

Northern harriers were once called marsh hawks because they hunt over marshes and meadows. They fly very slowly, low to the ground, and can hover over one spot, zigzagging back and forth. They have excellent hearing and catch mice and other small animals by listening for soft noises in the grass below.

Unlike most other hawks, harriers make their nests on the ground. They prefer wide-open spaces and seldom perch in trees.

Raptor watchers identify northern harriers by their slim bodies, long tails, narrow wings, and the white spot at the top base of their tails.

Northern harrier

The Fish Hawks

The osprey's long, rounded talons are specially designed for holding onto wriggling fish.

An osprey's talons can close over a fish in ¹⁄₅₀ of a second!

The curved beak of an osprey is a useful tool for tearing into its prey.

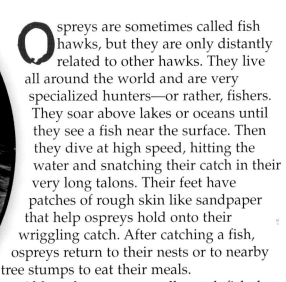

Ospreys are sometimes called fish hawks, but they are only distantly related to other hawks. They live all around the world and are very specialized hunters—or rather, fishers. They soar above lakes or oceans until they see a fish near the surface. Then they dive at high speed, hitting the water and snatching their catch in their very long talons. Their feet have patches of rough skin like sandpaper that help ospreys hold onto their wriggling catch. After catching a fish, ospreys return to their nests or to nearby tree stumps to eat their meals.

Although ospreys usually catch fish that weigh only about 7 ounces (200 g), some have been dragged underwater and drowned by fish that are too large for them to handle, such as salmon or sturgeon.

Home, Big Home

Osprey nests are easy to spot. They are made of huge piles of sticks at the tops of trees. Mating pairs will often return to the same nest year after year, adding to it each time. That's how some osprey nests get to be as heavy as half a ton (453 kg). Ospreys will build nests atop living or dead trees and will also use platforms made for them. In many places where trees have been cut down, conservationists have set up osprey platforms to provide places for the birds to nest.

An osprey soars.

Ospreys build huge nests of sticks. Some nests have been so big that they have broken trees!

Ospreys have feathers that are oilier than those of hawks and help to repel water.

Is there an osprey on the line? Some telephone companies have built platforms on top of telephone poles so ospreys will have a place to build their nests.

Ospreys can turn one of their forward-pointing toes backward so that they can grasp fish with two toes on each side, giving them a better hold. They also have long legs to help them reach into the water, but they're not afraid of getting wet. If they have to, they will dive into the water until only their heads show.

Eagles

Bald eagles prefer to live near water in order to be near the fish and water fowl they prey on.

Kings of Birds

Throughout history, people around the world have chosen eagles as the symbols of their countries. The Roman legions carried eagle standards, small statues of eagles mounted on poles. The bald eagle is the symbol of the United States. Of course, the bald eagle is not really bald. It got its name from the white feathers covering its head. In old English, the word *balde* meant "white."

Feast for a King

The crowned eagle of Africa can kill antelopes that weigh as much as 66 pounds (30 kg). The steppe eagle, also of Africa, which weighs almost 7 pounds (3 kg) and has a wingspan of 6.5 feet (2 m), feeds on termites in the winter. Golden eagles have been seen attacking pronghorn antelopes in Wyoming. The eagle flies fast and low over the ground, striking the antelope repeatedly with its talons until it falls.

THE GOLDEN EAGLE WILL ATTACK ANYTHING APPROACHING ITS NEST--*EVEN HELICOPTERS AND AIRPLANES*

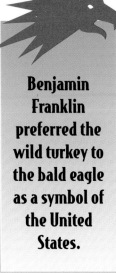

The bald eagle is one of the largest birds in America.

Eagles, Eagles, Eagles

The eagles of the world can be divided into four main types. Booted eagles have feathers that come down to their toes. They look like they are wearing boots. The golden eagle is an example of a booted eagle. Fish eagles, as you might guess, eat mainly fish. The American bald eagle is a fish eagle. Snake eagles, like the bateleur eagle of Africa, eat mainly snakes.

Forest eagles live in dense forests, often rain forests, in Africa, Central and South America, New Guinea, and the Philippines. There are six species of forest eagles, and they eat small mammals like monkeys. The harpy eagle of Central and South America is a forest eagle. Other forest eagles are the New Guinea harpy eagle, the Guiana crested eagle and the ornate hawk eagle of Central and South America, the crowned eagle of Africa, and the Philippine eagle.

The tawny eagle is a booted eagle.

Tawny eagles will often chase other raptors and steal their food.

21

The Eagle's Lair

Bald eagles build their nests out of sticks. They return to the same nests every year, adding more and more sticks. One bald eagle nest in Florida measured 9.5 feet (2.9 m) wide.

The vulturine eagle of Africa is called a fish eagle, but it rarely eats fish!

Eagles build their nests out of branches, twigs, and leaves. The nests can weigh several tons.

Extra Nests

Golden eagles in North America may have as many as 10 nests but use only two to three of them in successive years. Scientists don't know why they do this.

A scientist observes a golden eagle in its nest.

Duck! It's an Eagle!

Bald eagles have been known to hunt ducks in pairs. First, one eagle will dive toward a duck, which will dive underwater. The second eagle waits until the duck surfaces and then drives it underwater again. The eagles keep at it until the duck is exhausted and can no longer dive. Then one of the eagles catches it.

Bald eagles are part of the fish-eating branch of the family.

Gone Fishing

The osprey is not the only raptor to hunt fish. There are species of fish eagles around the world. Besides the bald eagle of North America, they include the white-tailed eagle found in Europe and Asia; the white-bellied sea eagle of Southeast Asia, India, and Australia; and the African fish eagle. African fish eagles resemble bald eagles except that their white feathers extend down from their heads to the tops of their chests and backs.

African fish eagles are noisy birds. They use loud calls to welcome their mates.

When Fish Are Scarce

Fish eagles will eat other kinds of animals when they can't get fish. Fish eagles that live near the ocean sometimes catch sea snakes. Sea snakes are not fish so they have to come to the surface to breathe. That's when the eagles catch them. The African fish eagle will also hunt flamingos and other waterbirds like herons.

23

Eagle Enemies

In the past, farmers and ranchers believed that eagles attacked and carried off livestock and even children. Eagles were shot and poisoned by the thousands. Today, we know that eagles do not attack people and only rarely attack livestock.

A United States Fish and Wildlife Service employee assists an injured eagle.

Monkeying Around

The Philippine eagle feeds on monkeys, squirrels, and other small animals. It eats so many monkeys that it's often called the Philippine monkey-eating eagle. It has a wingspan of around 6.5 feet (2 m) and weighs about 14 pounds (6.3 kg). Monkey-eating eagles have crests of feathers on their heads that stand up when they are excited or angry. The Philippine eagle is on the verge of extinction. It is estimated that there are only 300 left in the wild.

The Philippine monkey-eating eagle is the largest eagle in the world.

THE FEATHERS of an EAGLE WEIGH TWICE AS MUCH AS ITS BONES!

Harpies

The harpy eagle is named after a mythological creature that was half woman, half bird. It lives in the forests of Central and South America, where it eats sloths, lizards, and other small animals. Harpy eagles are probably the strongest of all the birds of prey. The feet of a female can measure 8 to 9 inches (20 to 23 cm) from front claw to hind claw.

The harpy eagle is the national bird of Panama.

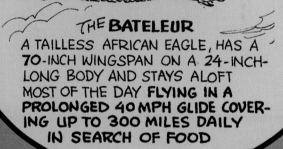

THE **BATELEUR**
A TAILLESS AFRICAN EAGLE, HAS A 70-INCH WINGSPAN ON A 24-INCH-LONG BODY AND STAYS ALOFT MOST OF THE DAY FLYING IN A PROLONGED 40 MPH GLIDE COVERING UP TO 300 MILES DAILY IN SEARCH OF FOOD

The word bateleur *means "balancer" in French. These eagles are acrobatic in the air, tilting and balancing on open wings from side to side, like tightrope walkers.*

Falcons

Mini Raptors

Falcons are the fastest-flying birds. Their wings are tapered and pointed for speed. Some falcon species are about the size of a pigeon. The smallest falcon is one of the smallest raptors. The black-thighed falconet grows to be only about 6 inches (15 cm) tall and weighs just 2 ounces (56 g).

A peregrine falcon looks around from its perch.

Hunter in Disguise

The merlin falcon uses some tricks in order to catch its food. It hunts small birds and starts out by flying slowly after them. Perhaps because the merlin flies slowly, its prey does not try to escape. At the last minute, the merlin swoops in and strikes with its small but sharp claws.

With prey in its talons, this merlin is ready for dinner.

Peregrine falcons are one of the most widespread birds of prey. They are found on every continent except Antarctica.

Some peregrine falcons that nest in northern Greenland fly to Argentina, near the tip of South America, and back every year. That's a round-trip of 18,000 miles (28,900 km)!

No Nests for Rest

Unlike eagles and most other raptors, falcons do not build nests. Some species, like the peregrine, lay their eggs on rocky ledges. Others lay their eggs in holes in tree trunks or even take over nests abandoned by other birds.

THE PEREGRINE FALCON AS A CHICK CAN TAKE AS LONG AS 2 DAYS *TO BREAK OUT OF ITS SHELL*

27

City Raptors

You don't have to travel into the wilderness to see peregrine falcons—there are pairs nesting on skyscrapers in cities all over the United States. The peregrines are at home in cities because the tall buildings and bridges are similar to their natural habitat on cliffs. Cities also provide a great food supply of pigeons, sparrows, and other small birds.

A peregrine falcon coming in for a landing.

Young peregrines often catch flying insects. Perhaps they are practicing on insects until they are big enough to catch birds.

This peregrine falcon and her chicks are living in captivity.

PEREGRINE FALCONS

which usually make their home on mountain cliffs and were becoming extinct due to poaching, predators and pesticides, are being released in cities to nest on the roofs and ledges of skyscrapers—and they are flourishing! About 36 have been released around Montreal, Quebec, according to McGill University ornithologist **DR. DAVID M. BIRD**.

The peregrine falcon's sideburns make it look like it's wearing a helmet.

One pair of peregrines, named Jack and Diane by bird-watchers, nested on a building in the Wall Street area for several years and raised more than 19 young.

A peregrine is eating its prey.

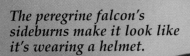

Falcon Teeth

Peregrine falcons have two "teeth" in the middle of their upper bills. These aren't really teeth like the ones we have but sharp points on its bill. If the peregrine does not kill its prey with its feet, it uses its teeth to snap the neck of the bird. Ouch.

It takes many birds to help a young peregrine grow. Scientists think that a family of peregrines needs to eat about 100 ducks or about 2,000 songbirds during their nesting season alone!

Hand-Trained Hawks

For thousands of years, people have been training birds of prey to hunt for them. The sport is called falconry, but hawks, eagles, and other raptors are also trained. The birds learn to take off from their owner's hand, kill a small animal or bird, and then return. The trainer wears a thick glove so he or she is not cut by the bird's sharp talons.

"It's all mine!" A peregrine falcon surrounds its prey.

FALCONERS IN medieval times WORE SPECIAL HATS WITH AN EXTENDED BRIM -WHICH SERVED AS AN UMBRELLA WHEN IT RAINED *TO KEEP THE BIRD DRY*

Falcon Furniture

Falconers use straps, metal rings, and other tools to hold and train their birds. They call this equipment "furniture." Hoods are placed over the birds' eyes to keep them calm until it is time to hunt. Today, some falconers attach radio transmitters to their birds so they can be traced in case they fly away.

The Falconry Weigh

Falconers know if a bird is ready to hunt by weighing it. If the bird weighs too much, it won't be hungry enough to hunt. If it weighs too little, it may be too weak to hunt.

A FALCON CAN SPOT A MOVING PREY FROM A HEIGHT OF 5,500 FEET

Bird Rank

In medieval times in Europe, only aristocrats could own some birds. The gyrfalcon was considered the bird of a king. Common folk could only own and hunt with birds of prey that weren't reserved for the nobility.

Today, falconry is a sport, but in medieval times, trained raptors were used to catch food. The goshawk was known as the "cook's bird" because it is a very reliable hunter.

Scavenger Falcons

The crested caracara is a bird that is closely related to falcons. It lives in Central and South America and parts of the southern United States, including Florida and Texas. Although the caracara does hunt, it lives mainly on carrion and seems to thrive on highway roadkill. It is a strong flier and can take off early in the morning, which gives it a headstart over vultures that have to wait for hot thermal air currents to form.

Vultures

The Cleanup Crew

Soaring high above the Earth, a vulture is often mistaken for a hawk or eagle from a distance. Up close, it is easy to see the difference. In fact, vultures in the Americas are more closely related to storks than to other raptors. Vultures do not kill their food but eat only carrion—animals that have died or been killed by some other animal. There are other birds of prey, including the bald eagle, that will occasionally eat carrion, but for vultures, it's their only food.

Vultures have excellent eyesight and can spot dead animals (carrion) from many miles away.

Bearded vultures are named for the bristly feathers that hang like a beard on their faces.

Weak-Footed Raptor

Of all the raptors, vultures have the weakest talons. Since they eat carrion, they don't need strong claws to kill and hold their food. Their feet are adapted for walking and for perching in trees.

A Running Start

Vultures like to soar on thermals high in the air. Their wings are very large, good for catching air currents but not so good for fast turns or takeoffs. That's why vultures have to take a running start before getting into the air.

Bearded vultures eat bones. They swallow the small ones whole and carry the large ones above rocky surfaces, dropping them until they shatter.

A jackal buzzard about to land.

In Africa, hundreds of vultures will sometimes gather to feast on the carcass of a dead zebra or other large animal.

Vultures gather for a feast.

A Bald-Headed Bird

Unlike the bald eagle, most vultures really are bald. Why don't they have feathers on their heads? Because when they eat, they stick their heads into the bodies of the animals they are devouring. If a vulture had feathers on its head, those feathers would be covered in blood and other remains every time the vulture ate. It is difficult for a bird to clean its own head feathers. The dirty head feathers would quickly attract insects. Not having any head feathers saves the vulture from having insects feasting on its head.

Lappet-faced vultures get their name from the lappets, or folds of skin, on the backs of their heads.

The heart of a turkey vulture beats about 132 times per minute. That's fast!

Follow That Vulture

The turkey vulture has a very keen sense of smell. Black vultures like to follow turkey vultures and steal dead animals they have sniffed out. Vultures watch each other as they soar in the sky. When one spots some food and drops down, others follow. This can set off a chain reaction, drawing vultures from as far as 200 miles (322 km) away.

A bird's eye view of Virgil, a turkey vulture. He lives at The Raptor Trust in Millington, New Jersey.

Vultures' long wings are suited for soaring.

Lend Me Your Beak

When smaller vultures find a large carcass, their beaks may not be strong enough to break through the animal's hide. If so, they have to wait for a larger vulture to arrive and start the feast. In South America, the king vulture is the first to tear open a carcass. In Africa, it is the lappet-faced vulture.

Vultures have strong necks and beaks to help them break through tough-skinned animals.

THE **WHITE-BACKED VULTURE** of Africa, HAS EYES SO SHARP IT CAN SPOT A PREY FROM A DISTANCE OF 100 MILES

The Egyptian vulture is the only bird of prey that uses tools. When it finds an ostrich egg, it picks up a rock in its beak and breaks the egg open.

THE CALIFORNIA CONDOR HAS A WINGSPAN OF **9 FEET**

The word *condor* comes from *kuntur,* the name used for the bird by Indians in South America.

King Condor

The largest of all birds of prey, condors are a type of vulture found in the New World. Once there were condors all across North America. Condor fossils have been found in Florida and New York. There were still condors in the East as late as 1800. Today, however, there are just two species of condor left—the Andean condor, found in South America, and the California condor, found in a small area of California. Condors have the longest wingspan of any bird of prey in the world.

Condo Crops

Like many birds, the condor has a special pouch used to hold food. The pouch is called a crop. The condor can store food there and digest it later. With a big meal and a full crop, a condor will not have to eat again for a few days.

The condor's crop, used for food storage, is visible as a bulge in its chest.

What's That Smell?

C ondors don't build nests. They usually lay their eggs in caves or crevices in cliffs. After several years of use, the nesting spot develops a very strong odor, thanks to all the bird dung and meat that builds up there.

The condor's beak is sharp and powerful enough to cut through a horse's hide.

Scientists have found fossils of a prehistoric condor species that lived 60 million years ago. It had a wingspan of 17 feet (5.1 m).

A California condor perches on a branch.

A **CONDOR** CAN CRUISE for A DISTANCE of 60 MILES, at 30 MPH, WITHOUT ONCE FLAPPING ITS WINGS!

The Brink of Extinction

In 1987, the California condor was on the verge of extinction. There were only 27 of the birds left alive. Although the condor has no natural enemies, people were killing it either directly or indirectly. Poisons and lead shot used against wolves and other animals were killing condors that ate the dead carcasses. The pesticide DDT, which was sprayed on crops, made condor eggshells too thin, so many eggs broke before the babies could be hatched. Loggers, farmers, and developers were destroying the condor's natural habitat. It was only a matter of time before the California condor would be gone forever.

A combination of government and private agencies worked together to try to save the California condor. All the remaining condors were captured and put in zoos. Scientists tried to get the condors to breed and produce eggs. At the time, no one knew if it would work, but today their efforts are paying off. There are now more than 200 California condors, and more than 70 of them have been reintroduced into the wild.

ALEXANDER DUMAS Jr.
(1824-1895)
WHO ALSO BECAME AN AUTHOR, FREQUENTLY TOOK WALKS WITH A PET *VULTURE ON A LEASH*

Puppet Parents

When a condor chick is hatched in a zoo, scientists use condor puppets to feed it. They don't want the chick to become so used to humans that it won't be able to adapt to life in the wild.

A baby condor accepts food from its condor puppet mother.

Biologists work with condors to help the species survive.

These condors are numbered to help scientists track them.

A condor study site.

OWLS

Silent Hunters of the Night

Owls are the only raptors and one of the few birds that fly at night. They are not fast fliers. They catch their prey by flying silently through the darkness. Unlike other birds, the first feather on each wing of an owl is serrated, like a comb. Owls' feathers are open and fluffy at the edges. This is why their flight is almost silent. They also have feathered feet, thought to better help them feel their prey and to help protect their feet from bites. There are about 140 species of owls around the world.

Owls are well adapted to night life. Like many other owls, the wood owl hunts at night.

Owl Eyes

Owl eyes are especially adapted for hunting at night, although some owls also hunt in daylight, at dawn, and at dusk. More than other raptors, owl eyes face forward, giving them very good depth perception. Their eyes are huge, and their retinas are adapted to see in very little light. The eyes of a great horned owl are about the same size as a person's, but a human being is about 50 times the size of an owl. That means an owl's eyes are much bigger in relation to its body.

The pupil of an owl's eye can open almost the entire width of the eye. Lots of light gets in that way.

THE OWL IS THE ONLY BIRD THAT LOOKS FORWARD WITH BOTH EYES

Great horned owl

Take a Look Around

Owls cannot move their eyes in their sockets, so they have to move their heads to see in different directions. By looking over their shoulders first one way and then the other, owls can turn their heads about 370 degrees. That's more than a complete circle, but they can't spin their heads around and around like a top. Unlike other birds, owls can see an object with both eyes at once.

Owls are the only birds that have flat faces and both eyes in front. This spotted owl has its eyes on you!

Mismatched Ears

The right and left ears on most owls are not exactly opposite each other. One ear is higher than the other, so when an owl hears the scratching of a mouse on the forest floor, the sounds reach its ears at slightly different times. This gives the owl a better sense of the distance and direction of its prey.

Like other owls, the northern spotted owl has keen hearing.

Contrary to what many people believe, owls are not blinded by daylight.

41

On the Day Shift

The snowy owl cannot hunt at night during the summer because it lives above the Arctic Circle. In the middle of the summer, there are 24 hours of daylight, so that makes night hunting out of the question!

A male snowy owl.

THE BIRD THAT RATTLES
WHEN RATTLED
THE SNOWY OWL (Nyctea scandiaca)
WHEN ALARMED MAKES A SOUND
LIKE LOUD RATTLES

The Edge of Night

Most raptors hunt only during the day, leaving the night free for other winged predators. This is probably why owls evolved such extraordinary night vision, sensitive hearing, and the ability to fly silently. They also avoid attacks from other birds, such as crows, which will often attack hawks and other predatory birds and try to drive them away or kill them.

The spotted eagle owl of Africa is a night owl.

COMMON BARN OWL

CATCHES MORE MICE THAN A DOZEN CATS

Don't Chew Your Food

Owls, like most birds, do not have teeth, so of course they cannot chew their food. Hawks, eagles, and other raptors tear their food with their beaks, but owls prefer to swallow their prey whole. They then spit up a ball of feathers, bones, and other parts they can't digest. These are called owl pellets. Other raptors also spit up pellets. Scientists study them to understand what the birds like to eat.

Say What, Saw-Whet?

The saw-whet owl gets its name from its repeated calls, which sound like a large saw being sharpened. (To whet a blade means to sharpen it.) They repeat their calls as often as 120 times a minute. These small raptors are only about 7 to 8 inches (17.78 to 20.32 cm) high and weigh about 4 ounces (113 g).

The saw-whet owl's rounded head has no feather tufts, and its eyes are bright yellow. The saw-whet owl has a wingspan of about 20 inches (50 cm), yet it has somewhere between 5,000 and 7,000 feathers.

Short-eared owl

The saw-whet owl's eyes are very large in relation to its head.

The Pels fishing owl swoops down to grab small fish at the water's surface.

NORTH AMERICAN BURROWING OWLS LAY THEIR EGGS *IN ABANDONED GOPHER HOLES* AND REMAIN UNDERGROUND ON THE NEST *for 27 DAYS.*

Underground Owls

As you might guess from their name, burrowing owls live underground. They often take over tunnels and nests dug by ground squirrels or other small animals. These owls eat insects, such as dragonflies and grasshoppers, and they catch insects while flying. Sometimes they catch and eat small rodents like mice and young prairie dogs. Burrowing owls are found in the western United States, Florida, and Central and South America.

Frozen Food

During the winter, some owls, including the great horned owl, will bury extra food in the snow. The meat freezes, and when the owl returns a day or two later, it thaws the food by sitting on it.

Burrowing owl

A great horned owl chick waits for its next meal.

Tiny Owls

There are three species of tiny owls found in North and Central America, and they are among the smallest raptors in the world. The northern pygmy owl has a wingspan of 12 inches (30 cm) and weighs about 2.5 ounces (70 g). It often hunts birds in daylight. The elf owl, found in parts of Arizona, New Mexico, Texas, and Mexico, has a wingspan of 13 inches (33 cm) and weighs only 1.4 ounces (40 g). That's less than a robin! It eats insects and is one of the few owls that hunts mainly during the day.

Northern pygmy owls are among the smallest raptors.

Pygmy owls fly by day as well as at night.

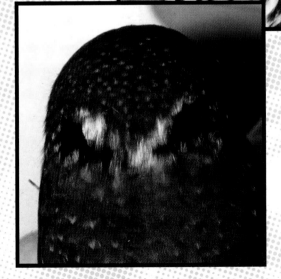

Spots on the back of the northern pygmy owl's head look like eyes!

Eyes in the Backs of Their Heads

The northern pygmy owl has "eyes," which are really black spots in its feathers, on the back of its head. This fools a predator into thinking that the tiny owl is watching it and discourages the predator from attacking.

Screech!

One of the most familiar owls in the eastern and central part of North America is the eastern screech owl. No, this small owl doesn't really screech, but its spooky call—a shrill whinny—might just give you the creeps. The eastern screech owl can be found in parks and wooded areas and even in backyards with large trees.

The western screech owl may look like its eastern relative; however, it sounds quite different. Western screech owls let out a series of bouncing whistles. They do not migrate but prefer to stay put. In fact, a western screech owl might be content to hang around the same place for months at a time.

Most screech owls, like this western screech owl, make their nests in natural tree hollows or in the deserted nests of other birds.

Can you find me? An eastern screech owl is nicely camouflaged in a tree.

A barn owl faces a human friend.

Barn owls can hear a mouse's footsteps from 100 feet (30.48 m) away.

Barn Owls' Ways

As their name suggests, barn owls tend to make their homes in human structures—such as silos, water tanks, and barns. Barn owls have such extraordinary hearing that they can catch mice they cannot even see. Scientists have tested barn owls in absolute pitch-dark rooms and found they were 100 percent accurate in nabbing mice in total darkness.

Barn owls develop a memory "sound map" of their hunting territory. This includes the auditory features of the landscape, such as the sounds of leaves, grasses, and water. The map even includes a memory of the sounds made by the creatures that live there.

Barn owls, with their pale underwings and bellies and their tendency to emit unearthly screams and screeches at night, have contributed to ghost stories worldwide.

Resources for Raptors

Raptors in Trouble

Most birds of prey have no natural enemies. The only danger to their existence comes from human beings. Until recently, people misunderstood raptors. Hawks, eagles, and falcons were seen as pests. They were shot, trapped, and poisoned by farmers and ranchers who thought they killed livestock. People also collected their eggs or shot them for sport.

People kill raptors even when they don't mean to. Condors and other birds die when they fly into electrical wires or eat lead shot in dead animals. Development takes away important habitat and nesting areas. As forests around the world are cut down, eagles, hawks, owls, and other birds of prey are losing their homes.

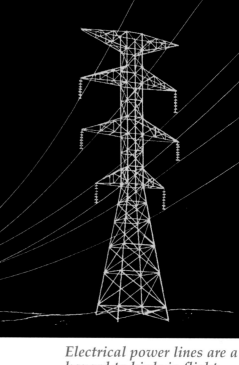

Electrical power lines are a hazard to birds in flight.

DDT

One of the biggest threats to raptors and other birds was the pesticide called DDT, which was sprayed on crops to kill insects. Birds and small animals ate the insects. The birds and small animals were then eaten by birds of prey, and a lot of DDT became concentrated in their bodies. No one knew it at first, but DDT makes eggshells too thin. When eagles or other birds sat on their eggs, the eggs broke. Because of DDT nearly all peregrine falcons and bald eagles in the eastern United States disappeared. Today, DDT is banned in most of the world, but the damage has had lasting effects on many birds.

Because of DDT, peregrine falcons nearly disappeared entirely from the United States.

Hawk Mountain

Hawk Mountain in Pennsylvania used to be a deadly spot for raptors. Thousands of migrating hawks and other birds were shot there every year. In 1934, the mountain was bought by bird lovers and turned into a sanctuary. Today, people flock to Hawk Mountain to watch birds and to shoot them—but only with cameras, not guns.

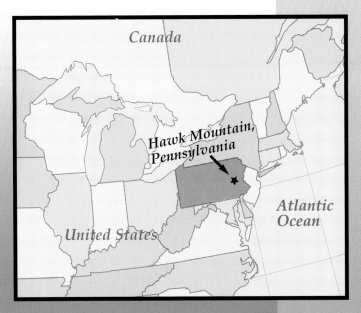

Canada

Hawk Mountain, Pennsylvania

United States

Atlantic Ocean

Bringing Back the Raptors

In 1970, scientists at Cornell University began one of the first programs to save raptors. The Peregrine Fund grew out of their work. It is one of the groups trying to reintroduce falcons, eagles, and other birds of prey to areas where they have died out. For example, bald eagles had almost disappeared from the eastern United States, but today they have come back to the East as well as many other places across the United States, from southern California to Maine.

Peregrine chicks wait for their next meal.

49

Caring for Eggs

O ne way conservationists introduce baby raptors to the wild is called hacking, and it involves raising baby birds in captivity. Scientists take the raptors' eggs, incubate them, and hatch them in a sheltered environment. This is useful if the eggshells are too thin to be tended by the parents or if the formerly captive parents don't know how to care for young birds. Scientists can keep the eggs warm without breaking them. Then the chicks can be placed in another nest or "hacked."

When a young bird is hacked, it is placed in a large box, called a hack box, where it is fed and sheltered with other young birds. Gradually, as the bird learns to hunt for itself, it is given less food. After a few weeks, the bird becomes independent of people and is ready to live in the wild.

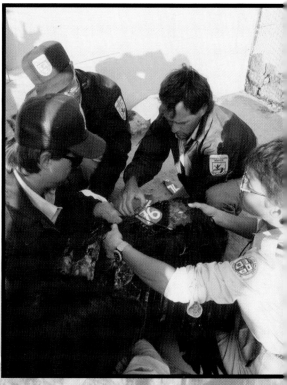

Conservationists tag raptors to track them while they are being cared for.

A Department of Fish and Wildlife employee checks condor eggs.

Rehab for Raptors

What happens to a bird that gets injured or to a young raptor that is orphaned? Without parents, how does it learn what it needs to know to survive? If an injured or an orphaned bird is fortunate, it will come into the hands of wildlife rehabilitators who specialize in caring for raptors. Rehabilitators in the United States must have permits from their state and the federal government to care for wildlife.

Most veterinarians are not equipped to handle birds of prey. Wild birds have very specific needs. The goal in wildlife rehabilitation is to return healthy wild animals to their natural habitat.

Orphaned raptors must rely on a combination of the rehabilitator's skills and their own natural instincts to successfully return to the wild. They have to know how to survive on their own. No one is going to be there to help them once they leave the protection of the center. Skilled rehabilitators do all they can to arm the animals with the information and skills they need to survive on their own.

To be a good wildlife rehabilitator requires more than loving animals. He or she must respect the wild one and know about its biology and medical needs to make sure it is well prepared to survive as a wild creature without further intervention from people.

A successful rehabilitation: A red-tailed hawk is released back to the wild.

A wildlife biologist and bald eagle share a quiet moment.

Backyard Conservation

Many birds of prey are poisoned unintentionally. Sometimes people place mouse or rat poison outside their homes. Various animals eat the poison, including squirrels, opossums, chipmunks, and stray cats as well as the mice and rats. Then, if these animals are eaten by predators, such as hawks and owls, they, too, will die.

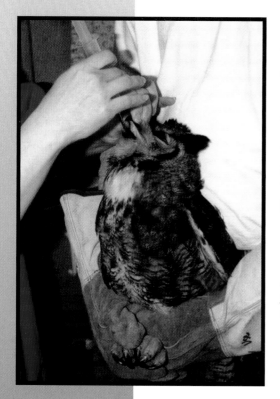

A dehydrated great horned owl gets fluids.

These great horned owl orphans are being cared for at The Raptor Trust in Millington, New Jersey.

SOS for Injured Birds

If you should come across an injured bird—a raptor or any other kind—there are a few things you should keep in mind. First, get an adult to help you. Next, do not handle the bird without getting the correct advice. Find the appropriate organization to get instructions on exactly what you or an adult should do. The organization may send a representative to help the bird.

Your best source of help is a wildlife or avian rehabilitator. Call your state's Department of Fish and Wildlife or try the Internet for a list of avian rehabilitators near your home. While animal shelters are wonderful for taking care of injured dogs, cats, and other animals, they are not equipped to handle raptors.

Raptors Around the World

Today, conservationists and scientists are working around the world to save birds of prey from extinction. There have been some successes, like the peregrine falcon and the bald eagle. The white-tailed sea eagle is making a comeback in Great Britain. Other birds are facing serious threats. The harpy eagle of South America and the Philippine eagle are two of the world's most endangered species. Efforts are being made to breed these birds and help them survive. It's up to all of us to make sure these magnificent hunters of the sky continue to soar overhead for years to come.

A California condor, the rarest North American bird of prey.

Because of conservation efforts, condors are making a comeback.

Discover More About Birds of Prey

Raptors are remarkable. If you would like to read more about these fascinating birds, here are some books that you might enjoy.

The Audubon Society Encyclopedia of North American Birds by John K. Terres. Wings Books, 1991.

The Bald Eagle Returns by Dorothy Hinshaw Patent. Clarion Books, 2000.

Birds of Prey, A Look at Daytime Raptors by Sneed B. Collard III. Franklin Watts, Grolier, 1999.

Book of North American Owls by Leen Roney Sattle. Clarion Books, 1995.

California Condors by Patricia A. Fink Martin. Children's Press, 2002.

The Condor by Lisa Westberg Peters. Crestwood House, 1990.

Eagles by Aubrey Lang. Sierra Club Wildlife Library, Little Brown and Company, 1990.

Eagles and Birds of Prey by Jemina Parry-Jones. Dorling Kindersley, 1997.

Eagles, Hawks, and Falcons of the World by Leslie Brown and Dean Amadon. The Wellfleet Press, 1989.

The Enchanting Owl by Connie Topps. Voyaguer Press, 1990.

The Great Gray Owl, Phantom of the Northern Forest by Robert W. Nero. Smithsonian Institution Press, 1980.

Hawk Highway in the Sky by Caroline Arnold. Harcourt Brace & Company, 1997.

How to Spot an Owl by Patricia Taylor Sutton and Clay Sutton. Chapters Publishing Ltd., 1994.

How to Spot Hawks & Eagles by Clay Sutton and Patricia Taylor Sutton. Chapters Publishing Ltd., 1996.

The Magnificent Birds of Prey by Phillip S. Callahan. Holiday House, 1974.

Osprey by Dorothy Hinshaw Patent. Clarion Books, 1993.

Owls, The Silent Fliers by R. D. Lawrence. Firefly Books, 2001.

Owls and Other Birds of Prey by Mary E. Reid. World Book, Inc., 2000.

Owls, Their Life and Behavior by Julie De La Torre. Crown Publishers, Inc., 1990.

Owls: Who Are They? by Kila Jarvis and Denver W. Holt. Mountain Press, 1996.

Raptor! by Christyna M. and Rene Laubach and Charles W. G. Smith. Storey Books, 2002.

The Sibley Guide to Bird Life and Behavior edited by Chris Elphick, John B. Dunning, Jr., and David Allen Sibley. Alfred A. Knopf, 2001.

See Live Raptors!

The following places have live raptors on-site and also provide information about these fascinating birds. Write or call to get specific information about the birds present, hours of operation, and other services, incuding education programs.

California
The Wildlife Waystation
14831 Little Tujunga Canyon Road
Angeles National Forest, CA 91342
(818) 899-5201

Colorado
Greenwood Wildlife Rehabilitation
Sanctuary
P.O. Box 18987
Boulder, CO 80308
(303) 545-5849

Georgia
Ellijay Wildlife Rehabilitation
Sanctuary
435 Cougar Lane
Ellijay, GA 30540
(706) 276-2980

Minnesota
Audubon Center of the North Woods
P.O. Box 530
Sandstone, MN 55072
(320) 245-2648

Missouri
Clarksville Nature Awareness Center
Clarksville, MO 63336
(573) 242-3132

New Jersey
The Raptor Trust
1390 White Bridge Road
Millington, NJ 07946
(908) 647-2353

New York
Berkshire Bird Paradise
43 Red Pond Road
Petersburgh, NY 12138
(518) 279-3801

North Carolina
The Carolina Raptor Center
P.O. Box 16443
Charlotte, NC 28297
(704) 875-6521

Oregon
Cascades Raptor Center
P.O. Box 5386
Eugene, OR 97405
(541) 485-1320

Vermont
Vermont Raptor Center
Vermont Institute of Natural Sciences
27023 Church Hill Road
Woodstock, VT 05091
(802) 457-2779

Glossary

accipiter A group of small to medium-sized hawks with shorter, rounded wings. They often fly low to the ground among trees.

buteo A group of hawks with broad wings and fan-shaped tails that usually soar high in the sky.

camouflage Protective coloring in animals and birds that help the animal to blend in with its surroundings.

carcass The dead body of an animal.

carrion The remains of a dead animal. Vultures eat only carrion.

conservationists Scientists or political activists who work to preserve natural environments like forests or oceans.

depth perception The ability to tell how far you are from an object. A person or animal needs two eyes in order to have good depth perception.

diurnal animals Animals that are active during the day and sleep at night.

extinction When a species or type of animal no longer exists.

falconry The sport of training falcons and other birds of prey to hunt as directed by humans.

food chain Every animal in an environment depends on other animals or plants as a food source. The order of which one eats what is called a food chain.

glide The action of a bird flying downward without flapping its wings.

habitat The type of place in which an animal or plant lives or grows. For example, ospreys live in habitats near water.

hacking A method for introducing young birds of prey into the wild.

nictitating membrane An "extra" lower eyelid that can quickly cover the entire eye to protect it.

nocturnal animals Animals that are active during the night and sleep during the day.

owl pellet The remains of a meal spit up by an owl. The pellets contain bones, feathers, and parts of the animal the owl can't digest.

pesticide A chemical poison used to kill insects, often used by farmers to protect their crops.

plucking post A tree stump or rock where a bird of prey sits to clean its kill before bringing it to the nest.

predators Animals that hunt and kill other animals for food.

prey Animals that are hunted for food by other animals.

raptor A term for a bird of prey.

soar The action of a bird flying without flapping its wings. It usually means the bird is flying in spirals on rising air.

spicule Spiny skin on the bottom of some raptors' feet.

talon A claw.

thermal An upward current of warm air. Many hawks, vultures, and other birds ride into the air on thermal currents.

trait A feature that an animal has that distinguishes it from other animals.

wingspan The distance from one wingtip of a bird to the other.

Index

Photo Credits

t=top   tl=top left   tr=top right
tm=top middle   m=middle   ml=middle left
mr=middle right   b=bottom   bl=bottom left
br= bottom right